MW00905396

RESTORING the WICKEDNESS

RESTORING
the WICKEDNESS

Eva Tihanyi

THISTLEDOWN PRESS

© 2000, Eva Tihanyi
All rights reserved

No part of this publication may be reproduced or transmitted in any form or by
any means, graphic, electronic or mechanical, including photocopying, recording,
or any information storage and retrieval system, without permission in writing
from the publisher.

Canadian Cataloguing in Publication Data

Tihanyi, Eva, 1956 –
Restoring the wickedness
Poems.
ISBN 1-894345-10-X
I. Title.
PS8589.I53 R48 2000   C811'.54   C00-920059-2
PR9199.3.T54 R48 2000

Cover painting *Mooncycles* by Barbara Bickel
Mixed media drawing on wood

Typeset by Thistledown Press Ltd.
Printed and bound in Canada

Thistledown Press Ltd.
633 Main Street
Saskatoon, Saskatchewan
S7H 0J8

Canadian   Patrimoine
Heritage   canadien

Thistledown Press gratefully acknowledges the financial assistance of the Canada
Council for the Arts, the Saskatchewan Arts Board, and the Government of
Canada through the Book Publishing Industry Development Program for its
publishing program.

ACKNOWLEDGEMENTS

Some of these poems have been published in *Books in Canada*, *Fireweed*, *The New Quarterly*, *The Windsor Review*, *Diviners*, *Room of One's Own*, *CALL*, *The Ottawa Citizen*, *The Literary Review of Canada*, *The Harpweaver*, *Forum*, *90 Poets for the Nineties* (anthology), *Vintage 96* (anthology), and *Vintage 2000* (anthology).

The list in "Wickedness" is from *The Synonym Finder* by J. J. Rodale (Rodale Press, 1978).

The quote in "Sunlight on Water" is from Diane Ackerman's *A Natural History of the Senses* (Vintage, 1990).

Thanks to all the "wicked women" who helped in the soul process, most especially Dianne, Darlene, Ricki, and Kim. (And to Martin for enduring the sometimes painful alchemy.)

Thanks also to Patricia Abram for her valuable comments on the manuscript.

And a special thank-you to Susan Musgrave for her insightful "fine tuning."

CONTENTS

EVERYTHING OLD IS NEW AGAIN

LET US PREPARE MYTHOLOGIES

COMMITTING LOVE

This one's for Brendan

EVERYTHING OLD IS NEW AGAIN

WICKEDNESS

Iniquity, evil, vice, improbity, sin, sinfulness, deviltry, ungodliness, godlessness, irreverence, impiety, irreligiousness, nefariousness, flagitiousness, heinousness, vileness, viciousness, badness, baseness, foulness, meanness, opprobrium, ignominy, disgrace, infamy, atrocity, outrage, abomination, enormity, crime, malefaction, wrongdoing, feloniousness, lawlessness, unregeneracy, impenitence, incorrigibility, maleficence, malignancy, malevolence, malignity, rancour, maliciousness, perfidy, treachery, foul play, villainy, knavery, rascality, delinquency, depravity, turpitude, degradation, degeneracy, corruption, pollution, profligacy, reprobacy, reprobateness, immorality, obliquity, immodesty, impudicity, indecency, debauchery, lewdness, lasciviousness, licentiousness, lust, lustfulness, venery, salacity, salaciousness, unchastity, promiscuity, concupiscence, perversity, bestiality, obscenity, profanity, bawdiness, ribaldry, vulgarity

Obviously a word with many meanings

You choose

LILITH ENTERS THE BOOK OF QUOTATIONS

Wicked women don't run with the wolves;
they are the wolves

MIXING THE MYTHS

1. NUTRITIONAL ADVICE

Baubo the Belly Goddess
in all her ribald splendour
plants herself roundly before Eve
and says:

Adam is a carnivore
though he doesn't know it yet,
but you're a vegetarian;
stop trying to be like him,
eat the apple and be nourished

But what about Adam? asks Eve

Baubo looks her straight in the eye

Let him eat snake, she says

2. THE DAWNING OF CONSCIOUSNESS

The beauty myth starts early,
back in the Garden
when Adam and Eve get jolted,
become suddenly aware
that fig leaves might be necessary

Adam, instantly critical
(this is, after all,
before the Men's Movement),
takes one look at Eve
and complains to God
that she is less than perfect
and what's the problem up there anyway,
has the Old Man lost his touch?

At first all Eve can do is blush

Then the apple takes effect,
and she wakes up

3. APPLE APPRECIATION

Intriguing, the apple;
so ripe with good and evil,
neither good nor evil

Although the serpent
steals the show, has the best lines,
the apple is more interesting,
a token fruit, small
but consequential

Yet no one pays
much attention to the apple,
how it felt in Eve's hand,
how it tasted on her curious tongue

And in the chain of blame
from Adam to Eve to snake,
it's surprising
the apple hasn't been accused —
simply of being there

4. ADAM'S VERSION

In the beginning, he is everything she wants, but she can't leave
well enough alone, starts tampering. Like a child with a paper
cut-out, she dismembers him: creatively and with good intentions.
At first the legs are too long, then the arms. Then the torso is too
wide and the head too large. More trimming, but the legs aren't
even. Soon there's nothing left but the box in the middle, the
essential square.

She mutilates him over and over, without thinking. For a while, she
is fortunate. Each time she cuts him down, he miraculously sprouts
new limbs, regenerates like an earthworm. But eventually, he can't
grow whole. His arms and legs stay stumps; his head emerges only
partially, a half circle.

No wonder he can't trust her when she puts the scissors down.

5. EVE PREPARES FOR THE 21st CENTURY

She needs new shoes, shoes
that will truly fit her

Running shoes
that honour Nike, that promise
the will to do it
whatever it is

The bland sales clerk, oblivious
to the myth now in progress,
asks what size

What she wants to answer:

Ask not what size shoe

Ask what size victory;
what size wings

LILITH'S ADVICE TO PERSEPHONE

Spit the pomegranate seed in Hades' face
and go home more often

ADAM'S WIVES

Lilith came first

She refused to lie
to him or beneath him;
she refused to lie at all,
insisted on standing

So he traded her in,
got Eve instead

Eve
took everything
lying down

Took it, that is,
until Lilith snaked back,
spelled it out for her
in one small bite

(One small bite for Eve,
one giant meal for womankind)

CONTINUING EDUCATION

Lilith hates with a hatred so pure
even Adam admires it

He respects direct rage,
the fist through the wall,
forceful and uncomplicated

What she wants next:
to teach him fear

EVE DREAMS HERSELF FORWARD

Reclaims the first person,
the embarrassing, naked I;
its guilt and need
and personal implications

Throws away the comb,
gives up trying to tame
her tousled life into order

Admits there are times
she hates God;
gets over it

EVE RE-EVALUATES HER NEMESIS

You remind me of the first Barbie,
the one in the zebra-striped bathing suit,
black open-toed shoes, white sunglasses

A fifties version of female perfection,
a black-and-white sort of girl,
small on brains, big on dichotomy

A quintessential corporate dream,
wet and profitable

Retro Barbie's back now, and so are you,
posed for the new millennium;
both repackaged in the zebra suit

I wonder if the future
can hear you mincing toward it,
whether it suspects the yes-no tap
of your high and mighty heels

LILITH TAKES UP RESIDENCE

Lilith, having grown tired of the desert,
decides to try Toronto,
see how the sisters are doing

And what better way than as a Barbie doll,
perfect disguise for a bitch
in a culture where
a Being In Total Control of Herself
is still suspect

So she arrives, accessorized to the hilt,
with talons and wings, owls and candles,
enough attitude to scare the Devil himself

An in-your-face Barbie
terrorizing department stores
in her *Better a bitch than a doormat* cape,
inspiring little girls of all ages
to be just like her

And Ken, poor Ken;
he suddenly grows genitals,
wants to get on top,
but of course she won't let him

BARBIE'S FATHER HAS A NIGHTMARE

His daughter, now 40,
decides she's had enough,
calls a press conference, announces
that like Xena, she will be
a figure of action, a warrior princess

Put simply, she wants to kick ass,
chide the gods as if they were
delinquent angels, predictable and delicate,
prey to her uncanny prescience

She wants to ditch Ken and teeter
on the highest ledge of pleasure,
dare her newly appointed heart
to commit a fall into erotic turbulence

She wants to indulge in choices of all kinds,
slide into black leather if she feels like it,
spike her hair, have Midge's name
tattooed on her breast, sport
an Athena countenance
as a conversation piece

She wants to dance with turpitude;
relish it

AT THE BAR: GIRLS' NIGHT OUT

Eve admits she's still
brooding over Adam, living
with her legs open, eyes closed,
mistaking blind sex
for blind faith

Persephone says she's finally
in love with Hades,
but he's no longer interested

Lilith downs a shot of tequila,
stays silent

Eve complains
she's bored with Adam, needs
more humour in her life,
more conversation

Persephone, near tears,
worries that *Hades* is bored with *her*,
doesn't know what to do about it

Lilith says this is why
she likes to fuck strangers

LILITH RE-CONVERTS A FORMER LOVER

She arrives unexpectedly
though I have been vigilant, forgetting
her body over and over, the way
it pushed against me,
pulled out lust, a wet spectacle
(that, too, unexpected at the time)

She's dressed in black as usual, leads me
across the bar to temptation,
and by the time we reach the farthest booth
I'm already beyond saving, have succumbed
to the onslaught of desire, the decadent sway
of her criminal hips, oh such tight denim

We slip into the dark corner, she into
my darkest recesses with her indigo eyes,
her gaze a silent erotic requiem
for all my safe loves, my havens of virtue

She is not safe, and I'm not sorry;
if this is damnation, then I'm damned,
an unrepentant reprobate

EVE SEES HERSELF MIRRORED

She now understands Narcissus,
how seeing yourself can be deadly

Irony: water is her element
but she can't swim

She looks into the still pool,
at the woman who is her, not her:
reflection, interpretation

Strangely, there is home in this,
a feeling of safety;
she trusts the water face, knows
that if she slips and falls
this woman will save her

That with her help
she will float, breathe, survive

A REVISIONIST VERSION
OF THE FIRST LOVE TRIANGLE

Eve and Lilith agree
it is stupid to fight over Adam,
grab a few apples for the road,
flee Eden

EVE FIXATES ON THE LETTER "A"

Divides the "A" words into nouns and verbs,
a simple linguistic dichotomy

Some — though surprisingly few —
fall into both columns,
androgynous words
shifting in their duality
like light
(particle and wave,
both and neither)

A finite list, definite;
orderly and alphabetical

> abuse
> act
> age
> air
> alarm
> anger
> appeal
> approach
> arm
> awe

She focuses on each in turn
until, under the spell of her concentration,
each hums itself like a tuning fork

> to abuse, to act
> to age, to air
> to alarm, to anger
> to appeal, to approach
> to arm, to awe

In the process she discovers something:
add a preposition and suddenly
nouns are no longer stationary, examinable

They move

LILITH'S SONG

Ravenous for self
as the raven is ravenous,
you are patron of chaos,
force of blood beckoning

Goddess of lust,
purveyor of wickedness,
you are the hazard,
the pre-guilt rogue element

Mother of demons,
lover of night boys,
you are the shadow
and wholeness demands you

PANDORA'S BOX

She guards it
jealously, won't let
just anyone
open it; pampers
and perfumes it, strokes
its oily surface
with pleasure

She knows
what secrets it contains

When she lifts
the lid, incorrigible
gifts take wing, pulse
against her body
with unexpected
ease

LET US PREPARE MYTHOLOGIES

" . . . I can no longer live with too much of a disparity between the outer expression and the inner belief."

— *Margaret Laurence in a letter to Adele Wiseman*

Who we are in what we live:
the army in the Trojan horse,
subversive, hidden,
larger than we think

Facade, the daily tasks;
truth is elsewhere

When it arrives, it will attack,
conquer without regret,
bear gifts

What then?

LANGUAGE LESSON

Surrender: sir-end-her

Homage: what is given to *les hommes*

Irony: nothing to do with shirts or mining

Common knowledge, that linguistic nuances
complicate matters, break
every story into multiple versions
all of which are true and false,
both and neither

What is less obvious: the process,
why we choose what we choose

Why, for instance,
we prefer *nude* to *naked*
or *lust* to *desire*

Why a man will call a woman
dear or *ma'am*

Why he might say *slut* or *bitch* instead

What's interesting
is not so much the word itself
but the reason it was picked

HANDWRITING

Hand, writing
Writing hand
Writing: hand

Right-handed
Left-handed
Backhanded
Underhanded
Have a hand in it
Hands up
Hands down
Hand in hand
Hands of time

Handout
Handmade
Hand-me-down
Hands on
Hands off
Play the hand
Handle

Handcuff
Hand job
Hand gun
Handshake
Shaking hands
Hands tied

Give me a hand
Hand it over
Hand me your hands
Unhand me

SHE CONSIDERS STARS

She considers stars, their coincidence

Had she been born Scorpio
she'd share a fate with Margaret Mead,
Madame Curie, Marie Antoinette

As only one of the three was beheaded
her odds would be good
for a long and heady life

She'd be a cornucopia of positive thinking:
if she broke a leg
she'd be grateful she didn't break two

She'd hold no false reverence,
would sculpt David
an erect and happy man

She'd be a gut intellectual,
aware of context;
would know every text is a con
and enjoy the challenge

In her version of the story,
it wouldn't be Icarus who falls,
but the sun — and Icarus
would be a woman

GEORGE FALUDY'S LIVING ROOM, CIRCA 1986

In a Toronto highrise
the poet sips tea,
his bold white hair
electrical as Einstein's

Next to his armchair: a live tree,
leafy and unexpected,
green with braggadocio
and brimming with finches
— sixteen in all —
that swoop and climb,
alight
on the whimsical branches,
try their song
against the walls

R.E.M. SLEEP, CANADIAN STYLE

Margaret Atwood rides a moose out of the bush. With one hand she waves, prim and queenly; with the other, flings blueberries the size of golf balls at unsuspecting Americans.

(The moose, its regal antlers branching like a tree, snorts its approval.)

Susanna Moodie runs after them shouting wilderness tips, while a grey-haired Gordon Lightfoot strums a rake, sings of maple leaves forever; and a grizzly,brandishing painted claws and a cellular phone, calls the Arctic; inquires about snow stocks, why they're falling.

Behind them all, Conrad Black shoots cash, hunts them down.

LADY CAROLINE LAMB

Odd, the implications
inherent in a name

More lion than lamb,
it is she who is mad, bad
and dangerous to know

She understands Byron
perfectly, sends him
a lock of pubic hair
to avow her passion

She's cunning
and unapologetic,
a creature of moment

When he leaves her,
she moans in her bed
thinking of him, hers
the animal soul
of a frantic dark princess

ANAÏS NIN COMES CLEAN

Believe me, it wasn't easy
A husband on each coast,
lovers in between
(Henry, June, two of a hundred)

A double life in multiples
each with its own costumes,
elaborate deceptions

A lifetime of paper worlds
penned with painstaking alacrity:
300,000 pages of journal,
the truth still nowhere

I was determined to be remembered

Craved immensity, mythic proportions,
the rush of ecstasy alchemized into art,
the greatest seducer

So I lied;
sue me

THE BIRTH OF FRIDA KAHLO

This was no immaculate conception;
it was messy and painful,
blood-bound from the start

Now, the miraculous coming:
I feel its will shifting inside me, sense
its animal hair and pagan teeth

I fear I might not survive
this newest advent of myself,
neither humble nor reticent

It does not falter nor prevaricate
as it rips its way forward

When its head appears,
it is serious and smiling

KINDRED SPIRIT

It takes one to know one,
and she recognizes him instantly:
a soul of hazardous intent,
well versed
in the dialectic of restlessness

And so she draws closer,
indulges her predisposition
to trouble and odd passions,
the entrails of beauty

Submits to his art,
a lust with no antedote

Like Duchamps' nude,
descends the staircase in fragments

Stills him
to absolute attention

How far down will she go?

In how many pieces?

RENAISSANCE MASTERPIECE

That's what she's become:
a piece of the master

Lisa del Giocondo, "La Gioconda,"
a Florentine merchant's wife,
the most famous
of all the canvas girls, her smile
a testament to the human heart,
its sad, equivocal whimsy

Leonardo, who loved her
best of all his work, infused her
with paradox, a sensual *sfumato*,
light and dark ambiguous,
forever intriguing

Now captive
behind a bullet-proof screen,
she is museum prize, icon of centuries,
a priceless face for viewing only

Imagine her then — and your surprise —
when she rises from her chair, shifts
out of pose, leaves the frame
frowning

JANIS JOPLIN WOULD HAVE LOVED YOU

Between your thighs:
horses, motorcycles, men

Behind you:
the hearts you've won and tossed,
their metronome devotion
still ticking

You abhor such smooth monotony,
demand a music fast and improvised,
tempting and savage

You're tall and unpredictable;
no one's going to talk you down

IDIOT SAVANT

He knows every position, every aid;
has memorized *Gray's Anatomy*,
The Joy of Sex and the *Kama Sutra*

He can name every bone and muscle,
recite treatises on the nature of breathing

His textbook definitions are impeccable

He can calculate excitement,
calibrate the heart

His precision is renowned,
his ability to arouse the body notable

When it comes to sex, he's a human hyperbole,
the perfectly perfect lover

Too bad he's no art and all technology,
weak on nuances, low on imagination

Perhaps if he learned Shakespeare,
he could interpret your eyes

DAUGHTER

Her father says
she doesn't act like one

Her husband says
she acts too much like one

Her therapist says
she is one
whether she acts like one or not

Her friends, all daughters themselves,
understand perfectly

As for her,
she's given up the role,
would rather be running

NOT EVERY WOMAN ADORES A FASCIST

It arrives in the mail: a useless provocation,
a stink bomb to the psyche, my father's
return address on the envelope:
my graduation photo, slightly creased
and battered at the corners,
no hint of explanation

It's my anger he wants;
a letter, a phone call,
any reaction will do

Which is why I'll do nothing;
have stopped trying to make truth
a lovable thing

As for propriety, I'll save it
for another life

It's time for the grown-up
version of the story;
the one where I refuse
to take the bait, live
not always happily
and certainly not forever after,
but on my own terms

KISSING

My grandmother's first boyfriend
was a blond, blue-eyed boy
with lips as smooth and sweet
as caramel

They'd go often to the train station
so they could kiss with impunity —
no neighbours, friends or parents,
just a station full of strangers
smiling at the two of them,
young lovers in the embrace
of greeting or goodbye

My grandmother laughed
when she told this story

*Anything is acceptable
in the right context,* she said

Remember that

THE STUFF OF LEGENDS

My grandmother and her friends,
all talk and teenage bravado,
laugh whenever they see him:
a trenchcoat man
flashing women in Heroes' Square

Except my grandmother,
who likes her words spiced with action,
decides one morning to maze her way
through the seemingly oblivious bystanders,
set on a course directly toward him

What happens next I can only imagine:
his startled look
as our heroine marches fearless,
determined
to flash her daring in his face

It's obvious
she'll grow to be the sort of woman
certain women frown at
and men underestimate

A FEAST OF SPARROWS

During the War, food was scarce
so my grandmother's father
caught neighbourhood birds

I've tried to imagine it,
the ingenuity, the skill, the method
of his trapping

Have wondered how many sparrows
it takes to make a meal

MY GRANDMOTHER REMEMBERS THE GABOR SISTERS

It was back in pre-glasnost Budapest,
before the rich husbands and American TV,
before the accent became a trademark joke
and joined *gulyás*
in the lexicon of Hungarian stereotypes

But they were theatrical even then,
and starkly ambitious;
took it for granted
that in an oyster world
they were most assuredly
pearl material

One friendly but too talkative;
the other arrogant, inflated
with aspiration

And both damned lucky
if you consider the times:
when they left the country,
only their mirrors noticed

IN THE BEGINNING

My grandmother's earliest memory:

> herself as a small child
> curled in her father's wheelbarrow,
> breathing the wind

IMPERATIVE

My grandmother lives out
the end of her dying

I swing back and forth
between you and her,
between the body's lust
and its demise,
the imperative of the body,
either way

The cruel air of the hospital,
the smell of semen on my thighs

There are many forms of love,
and each one is the hardest

MY GRANDMOTHER'S GLOVES

Even her gloves revealed her: soft leather,
not a common black or ordinary brown
but a deep flamboyant orange,
the rust of late autumn, warm and supple

They are the last things I have kept,
the final detritus after all the givings-away,
the ritual removals:
buttons in plastic pill containers,
assorted remnants of cloth,
zippers, needles, thread;
her clothes all gone,
her furniture distributed

Left: these exuberant gloves
I cannot bear to part with

For when I slip my hands into them,
I am held, perfectly

GRANDMOTHER

I want to restore you
to your wicca-dness,
your crone shape
pulled from the depths

I want to release you, shadow ally,
from stoves and dishes,
irons and needles,
the domestic domain
of your surface self

You were always a sly one,
beneath the daily tasks
a tamer of wisdom

You are now my myth
and my metaphor,
a bridge between
my face and the mirror,
the mirror and my soul

COMMITTING LOVE

BEGINNING AT ZERO

Zero is the most difficult number,
indivisible, heart
of all direction

Bring me zero
and I will show you a round riddle,
the hole into the looking glass,
everything and nothing;
an oasis of containment,
empty

Add zero to any number
and both it and the number will grow;
subtract zero
and it will make no difference

It even appears in *love*,
and *fool* has two of them

FOOL'S JOURNEY

Bliss colours the fields, and I, holy buffoon,
am improvising life, its song of amazement

To sing is to master the fear;
to sing is to own the desire

So I walk on through the light that golds the green,
joyous in my momentum, my unrehearsed singing

Around me: vines weighted with grapes,
trees festooned with apples,
the sky a triumphant blue

What has happened or will happen
is not what matters

Close your eyes and picture the world

If you can't imagine it,
it will never be yours

HARVEST MOON
For D.H. on her 40th

Every year
the vivid harvest moon
(no less mysterious
though men have walked on it)
lights the grape-heavy vines,
the apples on the verge of falling

In this moon's light
the world is less afraid;
the night cannot assume itself

I'm reminded of you:
how you, too, light
whatever comes toward you
even if it's heavy
or on the verge of falling

How when I draw near
I'm less afraid; for a moment
light as light

SUN ON WATER
For Patricia Keeney

Always
yours is a journey of engagement,
the "gorgeous fever of consciousness"
soaring within you, your breath intoxicated
by the scent of sun-warmed cedars,
your step marked by stones
pressing the soles of your sandals,
your ears tuned
to the hypnotic rhythm of light on water,
music made visible

When finally you pause,
you are fully in the moment;
momentous

Watch for hours as light
(original genius)
improvises on the river

Stand mesmerized into wonder,
your eyes welled with sight

WORD PLAY

My son, in third grade, is collecting nouns;
has decided he likes them

Giggle of geese, he says gleefully;
snide of lions

Herder of crows, I add, catching
the spirit of the game

Then, because I've always been prone to puns,
the worse the better, I command with mock severity:
Now let's play havoc

How do you play that? he asks,
intrigued and willing

Very carefully, I joke,
tickling him to laughter

What I don't say:
Ask God; he's the expert

FIRST FRIENDS

On a whim, I dig out the photo album,
the Grade Two class picture,
(black and white in those days)
and sure enough, there we are,
friends already
side by side in the front row,
locked into pose:
hands clasped in our laps,
feet crossed at the ankles,
both of us squinting at the sun

I don't remember this picture being taken

My earliest memory of you happens after school,
in your basement, in fluorescent light,
cool below-ground air

We play Beatles singles on your record player,
dance around the room and sing accompaniment
till from upstairs your mother hollers *turn it down*
and we giggle, pretend not to hear her,
while "She Loves You" accosts the walls
yet one more time

I look again at the picture,
your small smile, my wide grin;
wonder what moments live holographed
in the archives of your memory,
pedestalled to perfection

Imagine our child songs still sweet in us
though we're both past forty now
with children of our own,
teenagers in the basement
blaring their rap CDs
while we worry about them over coffee
at our respective kitchen tables

WHAT WE TAKE WITH US

My son plays soccer
in the summer rain, runs
across the keen grass
with the ardour of his age:
almost ten and timeless

Mud sticks to his cleats,
socks to his shins: his uniform
is soaked and clinging

Years from now
it's not the score he will remember,
nor whether he lost or won

What will remain:
the smooth wet nylon
against his back, the cool rain
on his hot face,
the power of his foot
connecting with the ball

HELEN'S ROOM

This probably isn't what Virginia meant
by a room of one's own, furnace at my back
and a poster (*The Lady's Not for Burning*),
grey walls hardly visible
behind the books and filing cabinets,
my sewing desk, the washing machine,
bulletin boards layered with must-do lists
grown musty

(All that's missing is the mildew,
but a girl can't have everything!)

A room in the underworld
isn't quite what I intended either,
but here I am, encrypted
with the mealy bugs and spiders,
closed in with my heart's stationary wanderings

Reminds me of a mausoleum, this place,
certainly a tomb of one type or another;
which means there are treasures too,
necessities for the during-life

What I cherish most: the gifts from my children,
rocks, driftwood, imprints of their childhood
like the hand my youngest gave me,
green fingers, red palm
pressed into white plaster

I survey the clutter:
open texts, papers at my feet,
notes scattered like landmines,
one small window only, sealed

I wish often for light,
possibly an explosion;
anything to help me breathe

But there are compensations:
frogs' bellies pressed against the glass,
field mice scurrying to their destinies,
thoughts about sky

OLD FRIENDS

Twenty years
since we last sat like this
side by side on a rock ledge,
entranced by the spring lake,
its blue abundance

Much has happened,
not happened

So far, we've survived
the large and small disasters,
continue to pick the Fool
more often than not, our deck
loaded with wild cards,
a Tarot for bohemians

Older now, but more reckless
in all the ways that count,
we marvel
at the sanctity of surprise, the way light
suddenly illuminates the leaves,
the beguiling presence
of what we have no name for

But still we search for names,
and that is what will grace us

I say: let foolishness be
our guide into life,
let the poetry spill off the page
back into the world from which it came,
an unexpected becoming
like Escher's hand drawing itself
into a hand

ELK LAKE REVISITED

When we arrive, there's a fire
raging behind Grady's Tavern

All afternoon it has been raining
but the flames continue, unappeased

The bar is empty,
the patrons gone either to help
or watch from close range

Tired from the long drive,
we nurse our beers, admire
the smoke's wistful beauty
below the lace valances

*I wonder if the head
is fooled sometimes, you say;
we come back to a place
and it reverts us*

I think of alchemy,
fire and water, transmutation; us
suddenly twenty years younger, reverted
by the simple act of being here
in this pared-down northern landscape

Memory is fickle, chooses
its moments at random; presents them
like water-perfected stones, surprising moons
among the dark debris

What we remember ignites us;
and like the phoenix
we burn down to what was
so we can re-invent what we'll be

BERRY PICKING

The berries grow larger, more abundant,
the higher we climb; at the hill's crest,
they swell in thick purple clusters like grapes

As we bend to pick them,
we blend into the August landscape, disappear
from each other like planes from radar,
call out occasionally into the silence
to register position

Long minutes pass before I catch sight of you,
rising suddenly to stretch, one hand
balancing a basket of berries, the other
pushing back your subversive hair

A perfect motion of rest,
the way you stand
for a moment in the moment,
being

Such pictures live on in us
long after the camera is lost
or broken or given away,
or simply no longer used

More than memory,
this photographic art

And more than art,
this form of love

FIRST MEETING

You pause for a moment in the doorway,
compose possibilities

I watch you, my breath quickening,
as you cross the room, navigate strangers,
traverse a lifetime;
enter my fate like a thread
through the eye of a needle

A word said over and over
becomes grace, an animal utterance,
profound and simple;
like *oh*, a note of wholeness,
a perfect circle of sound

Miracle   miracle   miracle

The word my soul hears
when you arrive

You, I say,
a sound as pure as *oh*,
as complex as desire

I pledge allegiance to your mouth

Articulate me

PEARL

It begins
with something miniscule but foreign,
a grain of sand perhaps

The oyster wraps the irritant
in layers of nacre,
continues this defense
until the granule is transformed
over time
into a soft gem, round and lustrous

It grows, a stone like no other

The earth did not conceive it;
heat did not harden it

Its light is warm,
its body smooth and self-contained;
it has no sharp edges

The surprise of relationship:
intruder as stimulant,
oyster as creator

You as particle around which
something lovely in me forms

I SEND YOU

I send you moonstones, shells,
my grandmother's embroidery
steeped in apple scent,
fragrance of cinnamon

Send you rogue stars, dream maps,
impossible blue roses,
my lexicon of paradise
lettered with affirmation

Send you white sheets,
miracles of potential
adorned with poems,
all the truths
I imagine I remember

Writing from the cusp of then and now,
I send you the future, for safekeeping

IN THIS DREAM

In this dream it is September,
a slow-motion afternoon, the two of us
sipping Merlot in the vineyard,
our heads sun-haloed, knees touching
under the weathered oak table

Around us, crisp edges of colour,
vines brimming with green,
the eyes of animals vivid
and discernible, in everything
the wild apparent

I reach over, guide your hand
across the smooth tablecloth,
teach its delicate braille
to your fingertips

Far away in the nearness
a bird warbles

Such focus, your eyes,
dark mercury
fluent with desire

You are safe with me

All I want
is to astonish your body
with love

CATS

I admire the two of them:
side by side on the kitchen floor,
sun-warmed, elegant as bookends;
no past or future, a perfect present only

I envy them this:
such stalwart impeccable wholeness

What I would give
for their fusion of time:
history and prediction simultaneous

What I would give
to curl on your deck like a cat,
alive in the heat of now,
caress of fur, your hands
so instinctive and intentional

CHOICE

So long ago: a kitchen doorway,
my roommate off to bed, you and I
facing each other
over Southern Comfort and cigarettes

I urged you to stay, sensed
that you would alter my growth
the way the wind does the shape of trees,
the way water re-contours stone

But I was renitent,
harder than I thought;
retained my essential configuration

It was the choice itself
that held the power, the moment
our lives intertwined, grew dense
like privets, branches crisscrossed,
leaves commingling

Over the years we've become
a wild but tender multitude
in which I'm still myself, though taller,
and much softer than a stone

A MATTER OF PERCEPTION

It was a matter of perception,
expected curves in unexpected places,
you behind the wheel, me
imagining bends where there were none,
certain they were there
even along the straightest stretches

I begged you to be careful: we were north
and it was winter, the road new to both of us,
a sly snake wending its way through the night,
tempting us with wrong turns, misdirections

I was afraid: it was late,
the threat of snow hovered,
and who were you really, this man
I'd just married?

But beneath the fear:
an odd faith in your vision, the power
of your eyes to guide us to safety,
to bring me home to morning
when I, too, could see what was real
in the light

GIFT

You pull my palm to your lips,
taste past and future,
your tongue tracing lifelines
slowly, so slowly,
it seems the earth
wheels a complete rotation

Gift: the way you touch
your lips to mine
as if you were religious
and this were a benediction:
two wings joined
in sudden astonished flight

PARADOX

Hot and cold:
the primal contradiction

To kiss you there
and there, here,
a roving heat,
a hundred small suns

To trail my tongue
along your throat,
cool trickle,
the merest of streams

Understand:
I love you most
when I don't have to

HANDS

1.

It: the universal pronoun of everything

She's not sure how it happens
but it does

She gives birth, becomes new,
a fresh version of herself
moving in a world more dangerous
yet more beautiful
than what it was

She balances lightly
along the invisible seam
between thought and word,
becomes once again
conscious of amazement

Is amazed by what
she still feels for him,
how in the beginning
she wore his dark love on her throat
like a cameo, like a hand

Now loves him more deeply
though depth is not always passion

Recognizes
that if this is a sadness,
so too is love

2.

Wonder: August,
lush and muscular,
clouds moving
against a plum and sinew night,
air heavy on skin,
palpable

She rolls it silently on her tongue:
plum and sinew, palpable
her mind pliant, plying through words,
hand through fur, feet
through long, soft grass

He stands by the window,
arms crossed, hands hidden

Dark sky, he says

Rain

3.

She waits in the cooling dark, watches
the clouds give way to stars, envies
the cat curled against his heart,
its trust instinctive as purring

It takes the warm rhythms of his hand,
gives back its pleasure

She, too, used to be able to do this
freely

In his hands she was a homecoming,
soul and body one

Now there's a faltering wedged between them,
a sudden virgule she can't turn
into a hyphen's small wisdom

Attempt at understanding:
futile as grabbing dust motes
in the curtain-filtered moonlight

All she knows: how much
she wants to write herself home
into his hands

IDEAL MOTION

Imagine the lamp on your desk,
the tension
of the taut brass chain as you pull,
order dark to light,
such power in your hand

Printed in April 2000 by

in Longueuil, Quebec